THE JOY I FEEL TODAY IS, IN PART, **BECAUSE OF YOU.** PRAYING YOU FEEL IT TOO.

May the God of hope fill you with all joy and peace.

ROMANS 15:13 CSB

Thankfulness is the quickest path to joy.

JEFFERSON BETHKE

DaySpring

Today I'm asking God to bring blessings to you front and center. Praying you see them, feel them, and appreciate them so much you burst *with joy.*

GIVE THANKS TO THE LORD,
FOR HE IS GOOD! HIS FAITHFUL LOVE
ENDURES FOREVER.
PSALM 107:1 NLT

I'm just thankful for everything,
all the blessings in my life, trying to stay that way.
I think that's the best way to start your day
and finish your day. It keeps everything in perspective.
TIM TEBOW

DaySpring

LIFE ISN'T ALWAYS EASY, BUT YOU'LL **NEVER BE ALONE.** I'M THANKING GOD FOR ALWAYS BEING BY YOUR SIDE.

And give thanks for everything to God the Father.

EPHESIANS 5:20 NLT

Faith does not concern itself with the entire journey. One step is enough.

LETTIE COWMAN

DaySpring

Praying in thanks for God's goodness in your life. You truly are *a blessing* to others.

I WILL BLESS YOU . . .
AND YOU WILL BE A BLESSING.

GENESIS 12:2 CSB

This is true faith, a living confidence in the goodness of God.

MARTIN LUTHER

DaySpring

TODAY I'M THANKING GOD THE WAY HE LEADS US THROUGH CHALLENGES. PRAYING YOU **FEEL HIM CLOSE.**

Throw yourselves into the work of the Master, confident that nothing you do for Him is a waste of time or effort.

I CORINTHIANS 15:58 THE MESSAGE

Often God has to shut a door in our face so that He can subsequently open the door through which He wants us to go.

CATHERINE MARSHALL

DaySpring

Praying you see *God's goodness* everywhere you look today.

**ARE ANY OF YOU HAPPY?
YOU SHOULD SING PRAISES.**

JAMES 5:13 NLT

Look for the goodness of God all around you. As you look for signs of His Presence, many more opportunities will occur for you to bless people and share God's true nature.

GRAHAM COOKE

DaySpring

THANKING GOD FOR YOU, FRIEND.

WHAT A GIFT YOU ARE.

The LORD gives His people strength; the LORD blesses His people with peace.

PSALM 29:11 CSB

When you're feeling grateful, look up—because God has again smiled on you through someone special who cared.

MATT ANDERSON

DaySpring

I'm asking God to *reveal His goodness* to you in a big way today so you know beyond a shadow of a doubt how much *He loves you.*

MAY THE LORD SMILE ON YOU
AND BE GRACIOUS TO YOU.

NUMBERS 6:25 NLT

Our heavenly Father supplies all our needs. . . .
He knows us completely, like no one else could.
God is the Giver of everything good.

NANCY COCKRELL

DaySpring

PRAYING YOU **SMILE MORE TODAY** THAN YOU HAVE IN YEARS.

God will supply all your needs according to His riches in glory in Christ Jesus.

PHILIPPIANS 4:19 CSB

It is not how much we have, but how much we enjoy, that makes happiness.

CHARLES SPURGEON

DaySpring

I am thankful for you, and today I'm making a point of telling God! Thank you for *being so wonderful.*

GOD . . . PROVIDES US WITH ALL THINGS TO ENJOY.

I TIMOTHY 6:17 CSB

A moment of gratitude makes a difference in your attitude.

BRUCE WILKINSON

DaySpring

PRAYING FOR YOU IN THESE CHALLENGING TIMES: THAT **GOD WOULD REVEAL HIMSELF TO YOU** IN BOTH BIG AND SMALL WAYS.

Give thanks to the Lord,
for He is good;
His faithful love
endures forever.

PSALM 118:29 CSB

No matter what our circumstances,
we can find a reason to be thankful.

DR. DAVID JEREMIAH

DaySpring

With a friend like you, it's easy *to be thankful.* Praying for you today!

LOVE NEVER GIVES UP,
NEVER LOSES FAITH,
IS ALWAYS HOPEFUL,
AND ENDURES THROUGH
EVERY CIRCUMSTANCE.
I CORINTHIANS 13:7 NLT

It is only with gratitude
that life becomes rich!
DIETRICH BONHOEFFER

DaySpring

ASKING GOD TO STRENGTHEN YOU WITH HIS JOY TODAY!

Pray diligently . . .
with your eyes wide open
in gratitude.

COLOSSIANS 4:2 THE MESSAGE

Anticipate the future and its changes with joy. There is a seed of God's love in every event, every circumstance, every unpleasant situation in which you may find yourself.

BARBARA JOHNSON

DaySpring

Praying you experience *the healing balm of laughter*—over and over again.

GOD BE WITH YOU!

. . . AND GOD BLESS YOU!

RUTH 2:4 THE MESSAGE

Gratitude brings joy and laughter into your life and into the lives of all those around you.

EILEEN CADDY

DaySpring

ASKING GOD TO BLESS YOU WITH EVERY FORM OF HIS GOODNESS AND LIFE.

I am trusting You,
O Lord, saying,
"You are my God!"
My future is
in Your hands.

PSALM 31:14–15 NLT

Every volcano is a powerful illustration of God's character. He is a Vesuvius of goodness, life, and energy.

REINHARD BONNKE

DaySpring

I'm praying that you understand just how much God loves you and that it fills you *with wonder and thankfulness.*

LORD, THERE IS NO ONE LIKE YOU! FOR YOU ARE GREAT, AND YOUR NAME IS FULL OF POWER.

JEREMIAH 10:6 NLT

The very fact that a holy, eternal, all-knowing, all-powerful, merciful, fair, and just God loves you and me is nothing short of astonishing.

FRANCIS CHAN

DaySpring

PRAYING FOR YOU TODAY, FRIEND. HIS GOODNESS IS ALWAYS PEEKING OUT FROM SURPRISING PLACES TO COVER US WITH HIS JOY.

God can pour on the blessings in astonishing ways.

II CORINTHIANS 9:8 THE MESSAGE

The Christian does not think God will love us because we are good, but that God will make us good because He loves us.

C. S. LEWIS

DaySpring

As you continue along your path, know that I'm praying for clear vision and an open heart for *all God has for you.*

NOTHING IN ALL CREATION
WILL EVER BE ABLE TO SEPARATE US
FROM THE LOVE OF GOD.

ROMANS 8:39 NLT

A mindset of gratitude
lifts the veil of bitterness and
allows you to see beauty and possibility.

STEVE MARABOLI

DaySpring

I HOPE YOU KNOW HOW VALUABLE AND BEAUTIFUL YOUR LIFE IS.

I'M PRAYING FOR GRATITUDE TO OVERFLOW OUT OF YOUR HEART AS YOU CONSIDER THE AMAZING LIFE THAT GOD HAS GIVEN YOU.

Don't worry about anything, but in everything, through prayer and petition with thanksgiving, present your requests to God. And the peace of God, which surpasses all understanding, will guard your hearts and minds in Christ Jesus.

PHILIPPIANS 4:6–7 CSB

Yesterday is forgotten,
today is in His hands, and
tomorrow is filled with His promises.

SUSAN GESELL

DaySpring

I'm praying you'll be comforted by ***God's faithfulness*** in your life.

He will never leave you!

THE LORD ALWAYS KEEPS HIS PROMISES; HE IS GRACIOUS IN ALL HE DOES.

PSALM 145:13 NLT

I have held many things in my hands,
and I have lost them all;
but whatever I have placed in God's hands,
that, I still possess.

CORRIE TEN BOOM

DaySpring

GOD'S PEACE BE WITH YOU TODAY AND ALWAYS. I'M PRAYING.

**And God is able
to bless you abundantly,
so that in all things at all times,
having all that you need,
you will abound
in every good work.**

II CORINTHIANS 9:8 NIV

Love, joy, peace, patience, kindness, goodness, faithfulness, gentleness, and self-control. To these I commit my day. If I succeed, I will give thanks. If I fail, I will seek His grace. And then, when this day is done, I will place my head on my pillow and rest.

MAX LUCADO

DaySpring

I'm giving thanks for you today and asking God to ***abundantly bless you.***

HE BRINGS GIFTS INTO OUR LIVES, MUCH THE SAME WAY THAT FRUIT APPEARS IN AN ORCHARD—THINGS LIKE AFFECTION FOR OTHERS, EXUBERANCE ABOUT LIFE, SERENITY.

GALATIANS 5:22 THE MESSAGE

It's one thing to be grateful.
It's another to give thanks.
Gratitude is what you feel.
Thanksgiving is what you do.

TIM KELLER

DaySpring

SOMETIMES IT'S HARD TO SEE THE BLESSINGS THROUGH THE RAIN, BUT THAT'S THE STUFF THAT RAINBOWS ARE MADE OF. **I'M PRAYING, RIGHT ALONGSIDE YOU,** FOR BLUE SKIES TO COME BACK SOON.

**Let your roots grow down into Him,
and let your lives be built on Him.
Then your faith will grow strong
in the truth you were taught,
and you will overflow with thankfulness.**

COLOSSIANS 2:7 NLT

We can see hope in the midst of hopelessness.
We can see peace in the midst of chaos.

PRISCILLA SHIRER

DaySpring

Thanking God for all the seen—*and unseen*—things He's doing in your life right now!

WE KNOW THAT GOD CAUSES EVERYTHING TO WORK TOGETHER FOR THE GOOD OF THOSE WHO LOVE GOD AND ARE CALLED ACCORDING TO HIS PURPOSE FOR THEM.

ROMANS 8:28 NLT

If there was ever a secret for unleashing God's powerful peace in a situation, it's developing a heart of true thanksgiving.

LYSA TERKEURST

DaySpring

I ASKED GOD TO GIVE YOU **A DEEP PEACE** TODAY—ONE THAT WOULD FILL YOU WITH JOY AND GRATITUDE.

Don't worry about anything, but in everything, through prayer and petition with thanksgiving, present your requests to God. And the peace of God, which surpasses all understanding, will guard your hearts and minds in Christ Jesus.

PHILIPPIANS 4:6–7 CSB

God is able to do what we can't do.

BILLY GRAHAM

DaySpring

Praying that God will take away all your worries and replace them with *gratitude and joy.*

TRUST IN THE LORD WITH ALL YOUR HEART, AND DO NOT RELY ON YOUR OWN UNDERSTANDING; IN ALL YOUR WAYS KNOW HIM, AND HE WILL MAKE YOUR PATHS STRAIGHT.

PROVERBS 3:5–6 CSB

In the happy moments—we'll thank Him.
In the busy moments—we'll bless Him.
In the trying moments—we'll trust Him.
In the quiet moments—we'll praise Him.

ROY ANDERSON

DaySpring

I WANT YOU TO KNOW THAT I'M RIGHT HERE WITH YOU, PRAYING AND TRUSTING AND CHEERING YOU ON!

O Lord, You . . . know
everything about me. You know
when I sit or stand. When far away
You know my every thought.
You chart the path ahead of me
and tell me where to stop and rest.
Every moment You know where I am.

PSALM 139:1–3 TLB

Gratitude paints little smiley faces
on everything it touches.

RICHELLE E. GOODRICH

DaySpring

I'm praying for you,
believing in you,
and wanting the
very best for you!

GIVE THANKS TO THE LORD AND PROCLAIM HIS GREATNESS. LET THE WHOLE WORLD KNOW WHAT HE HAS DONE.

PSALM 105:1 NLT

Thankfulness is an antidote to bitterness.

SUSAN GOSS

DaySpring

I PRAY YOU FEEL THE DEPTHS OF GOD'S GRACE AND THE BREADTH OF HIS LOVE FOR YOU TODAY.

Praise the Lord!
Give thanks to the Lord,
for He is good! His faithful love
endures forever.

PSALM 106:1 NLT

God's love is like an ocean.
You can see its beginning, but not its end.

RICK WARREN

DaySpring

I'm thanking God for His hand on your life, His arms wrapped around you, and His gentle voice *leading the way.*

REST IN THE LORD, AND WAIT PATIENTLY FOR HIM.

PSALM 37:7 KJV

When we put our problems in God's hands, He put His peace in our hearts.

ANONYMOUS

DaySpring

PRAYING IN THANKS

FOR THE GIFTS

GOD HAS GIVEN YOU!

YOU ARE A BLESSING

TO ME AND

SO MANY OTHERS.

And God is able to make every grace overflow to you, so that in every way, always having everything you need, you may excel in every good work.

II CORINTHIANS 9:8 CSB

God knows.
God sees. God cares.
Breathe, and rest.

TONY EVANS

DaySpring

Today I'm asking God to remind you how very much *you matter* to Him.

GOD CARES . . .

RIGHT DOWN TO THE LAST DETAIL.

JAMES 5:11 THE MESSAGE

God cares about every detail of your life . . .
He collects every tear in a bottle. (Psalm 56:8)
He numbers every hair on your head. (Luke 12:7)
He knows every hurt in your heart. (Psalm 34:18)

HOLLEY GERTH

DaySpring

PRAYING AS YOU DREAM BIG AND TRUST BIGGER! THANKING GOD FOR **ALL THE EXCITING ADVENTURES** HE HAS PLANNED FOR YOUR FUTURE.

If God cares so wonderfully
for flowers that are here today
and gone tomorrow,
won't He more surely care for you?

MATTHEW 6:30 TLB

Since it doesn't cost a dime to dream,
you'll never shortchange yourself
when you stretch your imagination.

ROBERT H. SCHULLER

DaySpring

Praying as you trust God *for big things.* Don't worry—He has it covered!

WE ARE MORE THAN CONQUERORS THROUGH HIM WHO LOVED US.

ROMANS 8:37 CSB

To be grateful is to recognize the love of God in everything He has given us—and He has given us everything.

THOMAS MERTON

DaySpring

TODAY I ASKED GOD TO HELP ME FIND WAYS TO LET YOU KNOW HOW MUCH I TRULY CARE ABOUT YOU.

God cares for you.

I PETER 5:7 CEV

Pray about BIG THINGS . . .
Pray about SMALL THINGS . . .
Because God cares about ALL THINGS
in your life.

ROY LESSIN

DaySpring

I love watching God work in your life. Today, I'm thanking Him for what He is doing *in and through you.*

FOR IT IS GOD WHO WORKS IN YOU TO WILL AND TO ACT IN ORDER TO FULFILL HIS GOOD PURPOSE.

PHILIPPIANS 2:13 NIV

God wants to do a deep work in us before He can do a great work through us.

CHRISTINE CAINE

DaySpring

I'M PRAYING FOR YOU TODAY—THAT YOU WOULD FEEL HIS LOVE, KNOW HIS JOY, AND **FIND A SONG OF THANKS IN YOUR HEART.**

With praise and thanksgiving they sang to the LORD.

EZRA 3:11 NIV

A grateful heart recognizes that all of life is a gift.

ADAM HAMILTON

DaySpring

I'm praying that you discover just how much *God loves you* today.

TEACH US TO NUMBER OUR DAYS, THAT WE MAY APPLY OUR HEARTS UNTO WISDOM.

PSALM 90:12 KJV

Joy is the direct result of having God's perspective on our daily lives and the effect of loving our Lord enough to obey His commands and trust His promises.

BILL BRIGHT

DaySpring

PRAYING YOU WILL BE OVERWHELMED **BY AMAZING BLESSINGS TODAY** AND EVERY DAY!

Every good and perfect gift is from above, coming down from the Father of lights.

JAMES 1:17 CSB

Gratitude unlocks the fullness of life.
It turns what we have into enough, and more.

MELODY BEATTIE

DaySpring

I'm asking God to show you, over and over again, evidence of His *incredible goodness* in your life.

TAKE DELIGHT IN THE LORD,
AND HE WILL GIVE YOU
YOUR HEART'S DESIRES.

PSALM 37:4 CSB

One grateful thought is a ray of sunshine.
A hundred such thoughts paint a sunrise.
A thousand will rival the glaring sky
at noonday.

RICHELLE E. GOODRICH

DaySpring

I'M PRAYING IN THANKS FOR ALL THAT GOD HAS DONE, IS DOING, AND WILL DO FOR YOU.

**You reveal the path of life to me;
in Your presence is abundant joy.**

PSALM 16:11 CSB

We are all on our way somewhere.
We'll get there if we just keep going.

BARBARA JOHNSON

DaySpring

You are unique in His eyes, *accepted*, and truly a gift. I'm thanking God today for the amazingness that is you.

BLESSED BE HIS GLORIOUS NAME FOREVER;
THE WHOLE EARTH IS FILLED WITH HIS GLORY.

PSALM 72:19 CSB

Be who God meant you to be
and you will set the world on fire.

CATHERINE OF SIENA

DaySpring

I THANKED GOD TODAY FOR ALL HE HAS DONE FOR YOU IN YOUR PAST AND **FOR WHAT HE IS PREPARING FOR YOUR FUTURE.** I PRAY YOU EXPERIENCE HIS GOODNESS ALL THE DAYS OF YOUR LIFE.

Surely Your goodness and unfailing love will pursue me all the days of my life.

PSALM 23:6 NLT

God, grant me the serenity to accept the things I cannot change, the courage to change the things I can, and the wisdom to know the difference.

REINHOLD NIEBUHR

DaySpring

Today,
I thanked God for
the many things
He is doing
in your life.

I HAVE LEARNED
HOW TO BE CONTENT
WITH WHATEVER I HAVE.
PHILIPPIANS 4:11 NLT

There is wonderful freedom
and joy in coming to recognize
that the fun is in the becoming.
GLORIA GAITHER

DaySpring

TODAY, I THANKED GOD FOR THE GOOD PLANS **HE HAS PURPOSED FOR YOU.** I ASKED HIM TO CONTINUE TO KEEP AND PROTECT YOU ON YOUR JOURNEY.

I will bless you with a future filled with hope.

JEREMIAH 29:11 CEV

God knows not only what we need but also when we need it. His timing is always perfect.

ELISABETH ELLIOT

DaySpring

I thanked God today for leading you through the tough times. I asked Him to continue to guide you toward *the best possible outcome.*

I AM THE LORD YOUR GOD,
WHO TEACHES YOU WHAT
IS GOOD FOR YOU AND
LEADS YOU ALONG THE PATHS
YOU SHOULD FOLLOW.

ISAIAH 48:17 NLT

Strive in prayer; let faith fill your heart—
so will you be strong in the Lord,
and in the power of His might.

ANDREW MURRAY

DaySpring

PRAYING THAT GOD'S FAITHFUL LOVE WOULD BE REAL FOR YOU TODAY, AND THAT IT WOULD BLESS YOUR HEART WITH THANKS AND PRAISE.

May Your faithful love rest on us,
Lord, for we put our hope in You.

PSALM 33:22 CSB

Gratitude is the ability to experience life as a gift. It liberates us from the prison of self-preoccupation.

JOHN ORTBERG

DaySpring

I prayed that you would experience *the fullness of joy* each and every day of your life.

YOU REVEAL THE PATH OF LIFE TO ME; IN YOUR PRESENCE IS ABUNDANT JOY.

PSALM 16:11 CSB

We can thank God for the simple gifts of grace He gives us every day.

SHEILA WALSH

DaySpring

YOU AND YOUR GIFTS, MY FRIEND, ARE A GIFT. I'M THANKING GOD FOR EQUIPPING **AND USING YOU IN WONDERFUL WAYS.**

God has given each of you a gift from His great variety of spiritual gifts. Use them well to serve one another.

I PETER 4:10 NLT

Our favorite attitude should be gratitude.

ZIG ZIGLAR

DaySpring

Asking God to show up in your ordinary and make your day *extraordinary!*

YOU ARE THE GOD OF GREAT WONDERS! YOU DEMONSTRATE YOUR AWESOME POWER AMONG THE NATIONS.

PSALM 77:14 NLT

Gratitude can transform common days into thanksgivings, turn routine jobs into joy, and change ordinary opportunities into blessings.

WILLIAM ARTHUR WARD

DaySpring

I ASKED GOD TO GIVE YOU A **REASSURING SENSE** OF SECURITY AND PROTECTION TODAY. HE IS INDEED TRUSTWORTHY!

Oh, the joys of those who trust the Lord.

PSALM 40:4 NLT

Replace worry with prayer. Make the decision to pray whenever you catch yourself worrying.

ELIZABETH GEORGE

DaySpring

I'm thanking God for your *joyful heart today.* It has blessed me so many times.

DON'T WORRY ABOUT ANYTHING; INSTEAD, PRAY ABOUT EVERYTHING. TELL GOD WHAT YOU NEED, AND THANK HIM FOR ALL HE HAS DONE.

PHILIPPIANS 4:6 NLT

Happiness depends on what happens; joy does not.

OSWALD CHAMBERS

DaySpring

I PRAYED GOD WOULD TAKE AWAY THE STRESSES AND STRAINS OF YOUR LIFE AND REMIND YOU **THAT HE IS THE ROCK,** THE SOLID GROUND, THAT YOU CAN STAND ON.

God is my helper; the Lord is the sustainer of my life.

PSALM 54:4 CSB

Faith does not occupy itself with outward things; it is an act of the will . . . an inward choice that says, "I believe, though I don't see. I trust, though I can't understand."

GWEN FAULKENBERRY

DaySpring

Today I asked God to remind you that His *care & faithfulness* stretch beyond the limits of time and space.

FAITH SHOWS THE REALITY OF WHAT WE HOPE FOR; IT IS THE EVIDENCE OF THINGS WE CANNOT SEE.

HEBREWS 11:1 NLT

God is the silent partner in all great enterprises.

ABRAHAM LINCOLN

DaySpring

I CAN'T WAIT TO SEE WHAT GOD IS UP TO IN YOUR LIFE. BUT I KNOW **IT'S GOING TO BE WONDERFUL,** AND I'M THANKING HIM IN ADVANCE!

So encourage each other
and build each other up,
just as you are already doing.

I THESSALONIANS 5:11 NLT

When we put our hope
and trust in God, we find that
His faithfulness is unmistakable,
His goodness is unrelenting, and
His prodigal love is constant no matter what.

JAMI PIERCE

DaySpring

What a treasure you are! I thanked God today *for creating you.*

MAY YOUR FAITHFUL LOVE REST ON US, LORD, FOR WE PUT OUR HOPE IN YOU.

PSALM 33:22 CSB

God does not love us
because we are valuable.
We are valuable
because God loves us.

FULTON SHEEN

DaySpring

PRAYING THAT YOUR HEART WILL BE OVERWHELMED WITH JOY FOR THE WAYS THAT GOD IS **CARING FOR YOU.**

Even the very hairs of your head are all numbered. Fear not therefore: ye are of more value than many sparrows.

LUKE 12:7 KJV

When trouble comes,
focus on God's ability to care for you.

CHARLES STANLEY

DaySpring

As I pray for you today, I'm thanking God *for hope.* We get to lean into every one of His promises, and that is such a blessing.

GOD IS OUR REFUGE AND STRENGTH, ALWAYS READY TO HELP IN TIMES OF TROUBLE.

PSALM 46:1 NLT

There is never a time when we may not hope in God. Whatever our necessities, however great our difficulties, and though to all appearance help is impossible, yet our business is to hope in God, and it will be found that it is not in vain.

GEORGE MUELLER

DaySpring

THANKING GOD TODAY FOR THE BLESSING OF YOU. HOW YOU SHINE IN THIS WORLD!

God can point to us in all future ages as examples of the incredible wealth of His grace and kindness toward us.

EPHESIANS 2:7 NLT

God uses ordinary people who are obedient to Him to do extraordinary things.

JOHN MAXWELL

DaySpring

Praying today that God's love would *overwhelm* and surprise you!

NO POWER IN THE SKY ABOVE OR IN THE EARTH BELOW—INDEED, NOTHING IN ALL CREATION WILL EVER BE ABLE TO SEPARATE US FROM THE LOVE OF GOD THAT IS REVEALED IN CHRIST JESUS OUR LORD.

ROMANS 8:39 NLT

We should be astonished at the goodness of God, stunned that He should bother to call us by name, our mouths wide open at His love, bewildered that at this very moment we are standing on holy ground.

BRENNAN MANNING

DaySpring

TODAY, I'M THANKING GOD FOR THE GIFT OF YOU.

By His divine power, God has given us everything we need for living a godly life. We have received all of this by coming to know Him, the one who called us to Himself by means of His marvelous glory and excellence.

II PETER 1:3 NLT

Every day we live is a priceless gift of God, loaded with possibilities to learn something new, to gain fresh insights.

DALE EVANS ROGERS

DaySpring

I prayed that new showers of God's *sufficient grace* will flood your weary soul today.

THE LORD WILL ALWAYS GUIDE YOU.

ISAIAH 58:11 CEV

When you experience the challenges of life, perspective is everything.

JONI EARECKSON TADA

DaySpring

I THANKED GOD FOR HIS LOVING-KINDNESS AND TENDER MERCIES TODAY. HE LOVES YOU **UNCONDITIONALLY.**

The LORD will provide what is good.

PSALM 85:12 CSB

Kindness is no small thing.
Trieste Vaillancourt

DaySpring

So many people have been changed for good by your generosity and love. Praying you feel the refreshment, joy, and blessing of God for *who you are and all that you do!*

YOUR KINDNESS HAS OFTEN REFRESHED THE HEARTS OF GOD'S PEOPLE.

PHILEMON 1:7 NLT

The care of God is certain, whatever we endure,
God's promise is unchanging to keep our hope secure,
His kindness is refreshing like sweet rain from above,
And life unfolds its purpose in God's unfailing love.

BARBARA LOOTS

DaySpring

TODAY I'M ASKING GOD TO REMIND YOU OF **THE GRAND DESIGN** HE HAS FOR YOUR LIFE. IT MAY NOT FEEL LIKE IT NOW, BUT TRUST ME, HE IS AT WORK IN YOU RIGHT NOW.

It's in Christ that we find out who we are and what we are living for. Long before we first heard of Christ and got our hopes up, He had His eye on us, had designs on us for glorious living, part of the overall purpose He is working out in everything and everyone.

EPHESIANS 1:11–12 THE MESSAGE

Thankfulness is a key to your life. It is the key that turns your situation around because it changes you, your outlook, and your attitude. There is power in a thankful heart!

ANN WOODRUFF

DaySpring

Friend, God has His eye on your path and His hand on your back, *gently guiding.* I'm thanking Him for what He is doing in your life.

BLESSED BE THE GOD AND FATHER OF OUR LORD JESUS CHRIST, THE FATHER OF MERCIES AND THE GOD OF ALL COMFORT.

II CORINTHIANS 1:3 CSB

Take courage.
We walk in the wilderness today and in the Promised Land tomorrow.

D. L. MOODY

DaySpring

PRAYING FOR YOU TODAY! ASKING GOD TO GIVE YOU MOMENTS THROUGHOUT THE DAY TO SAY, **"WOW! THANK YOU, GOD!"**

**Be brave. Be strong.
Don't give up.**

PSALM 31:24 THE MESSAGE

There's not much you can't achieve or endure if you know God is walking by your side.

BILL HYBELS

DaySpring

I'm so thankful to God for this day and *His willingness* to walk with us through it. Praying you feel *His hand in your walk today.*

THIS IS THE DAY THE LORD HAS MADE;
LET'S REJOICE AND BE GLAD IN IT.

PSALM 118:24 CSB

The truth is, God's strength is fully revealed when our strength is depleted.

LIZ CURTIS HIGGS

DaySpring

GOD IS THE GOD OF ABUNDANCE—AND TODAY I'M ASKING HIM TO MAKE THAT ABUNDANTLY CLEAR TO YOU!

God . . . will supply all your needs from His glorious riches.

PHILIPPIANS 4:19 NLT

Fill up the spare moments of your life with praise and thanksgiving.

SARAH YOUNG

DaySpring

Praying that God's *peaceful presence and reassuring strength* would be close and clear to you today.

BE STILL,

AND KNOW THAT I AM GOD!

PSALM 46:10 NLT

Don't be afraid to ask your heavenly Father for anything you need. Indeed, nothing is too small for God's attention or too great for His power.

DENNIS SWANBERG

DaySpring

THANKING GOD FOR THE GIFTS HE'S GIVEN YOU AND HIS PROMISE TO BE NEAR THROUGHOUT YOUR JOURNEY.

How we thank God for you!
Because of you we have great joy
as we enter God's presence.

I THESSALONIANS 3:9 NLT

"Little things" have big potential with God.

RICH DAVIS

DaySpring

I'm thanking God on your behalf for the ways He's making a way. It's going to *get better and better!*

NOTHING WILL BE IMPOSSIBLE WITH GOD.

LUKE 1:37 CSB

God knows what each one of us is dealing with. He knows our pressures. He knows our conflicts. And He has made a provision for each and every one of them.

KAY ARTHUR

DaySpring

PRAYING FOR JOY TO SURROUND YOU, GRATITUDE TO DELIGHT YOU, AND GOD'S LOVE TO BLESS YOUR HEART.

May Your faithful love rest on us, Lord, for we put our hope in You.

PSALM 33:22 CSB

If we fill our lives with simple good things and constantly thank God for them, we will be joyful.

RICHARD J. FOSTER

DaySpring

Today as I pray for you, I'm asking Him to *draw near to you* and bless your socks off with how much He just wants to be your friend.

THINK ABOUT THINGS THAT ARE EXCELLENT AND WORTHY OF PRAISE.

PHILIPPIANS 4:8 NLT

Don't allow the opinions of other people to shape your concept of Him. Get to know Him yourself, and let the goodness of God change you from the inside out.

JUDAH SMITH

DaySpring

GOD'S LOVE IS SO FAITHFUL AND HIS CHARACTER IS UNCHANGING. I'M ASKING HIM TO MAKE THAT SO CLEAR TO YOU TODAY!

His promise was true. . . .
His purposes never change. . . .
These things . . . give us strength
to hold on to the hope
we have been given.

HEBREWS 6:17–18 NCV

The more you believe and trust God, the more limitless your possibilities become for your family, your career—for your life!

RICK WARREN

DaySpring

I thank God for you *every single day*. What a treasure you are!

WITH GOD'S POWER WORKING IN US, GOD CAN DO MUCH, MUCH MORE THAN ANYTHING WE CAN ASK OR IMAGINE.

EPHESIANS 3:20 NCV

Do all the good you can, in all the ways you can, in all the places you can, at all the times you can, to all the people you can.

JOHN WESLEY

DaySpring

WHAT A GENEROUS, FAITH-FILLED PERSON YOU ARE. I'M THANKING GOD FOR ALLOWING OUR PATHS TO CROSS.

If your faith is as big as a mustard seed,
you can say to this mountain,
"Move from here to there," and it will move.
All things will be possible for you.

MATTHEW 17:20 NCV

The more you give, the more comes back to you,
because God is the greatest giver in the universe,
and He won't let you out-give Him. Go ahead and try.
See what happens.

RANDY ALCORN

DaySpring

Just look at you shine! What a bright spot you are! I'm thanking the Lord for how He fills you up and uses *you to be a light to so many.*

GIVE, AND YOU WILL RECEIVE. YOUR GIFT WILL RETURN TO YOU IN FULL—PRESSED DOWN, SHAKEN TOGETHER TO MAKE ROOM FOR MORE, RUNNING OVER, AND POURED INTO YOUR LAP. THE AMOUNT YOU GIVE WILL DETERMINE THE AMOUNT YOU GET BACK.

LUKE 6:38 NLT

If we magnified blessings
as much as we magnify disappointments,
we would all be much happier.

JOHN WOODEN

DaySpring

PRAYING THAT THE **GOODNESS OF GOD** WOULD OVERWHELM YOU WITH HOPE AND JOY TODAY.

Let Your people be happy and celebrate because of You.

PSALM 68:3 CEV

When we determine to dwell on the good and excellent things in life, we will be so full of those things that they will tend to swallow our problems.

RICHARD J. FOSTER

DaySpring

God placed you in my life at *just the right time,* and for that, I will never stop thanking Him.

THE LORD HAS BLESSED ME BECAUSE OF YOU.

GENESIS 30:27 NLT

God's power is great enough for our deepest desperation. You can go on. You can pick up the pieces and start anew. You can face your fears. There is healing for your soul.

SUZANNE DALE EZELL

DaySpring

I'M PRAISING GOD FOR HIS GOODNESS AND UNFAILING LOVE FOR YOU. THERE'S NO NEED TO WORRY! **HE WILL NEVER LEAVE YOU.**

Surely Your goodness and unfailing love will pursue me all the days of my life.

PSALM 23:6 NLT

Don't worry about tomorrow.
God is already there.

(IN)COURAGE

DaySpring

I asked God to remind you of *His amazing love* today. Nothing can remove you from His care!

I AM CONVINCED THAT NOTHING CAN EVER SEPARATE US FROM GOD'S LOVE.

ROMANS 8:38 NLT

From the heart of God comes the strongest rhythm—the rhythm of love. . . . And so the work of the human heart, it seems to me, is to listen for that music and pick up on its rhythms.

KEN GIRE

DaySpring

PRAYING THAT GOD'S PEACE **WOULD BE REAL** IN YOUR HEART EVERY DAY AND IN EVERY WAY.

May grace and peace be multiplied to you through the knowledge of God and of Jesus our Lord.

II PETER 1:2 CSB

Just hang on—God's got a grand view in His plan for you!

JULIE SAWYER

DaySpring

As I pray for you today, I'm asking Him to show you a glimpse of His plan and *the valuable ways* you add your own personal spark to it!

YOU, LORD GOD, HAVE DONE MANY WONDERFUL THINGS, AND YOU HAVE PLANNED MARVELOUS THINGS FOR US. NO ONE IS LIKE YOU! I WOULD NEVER BE ABLE TO TELL ALL YOU HAVE DONE.

PSALM 40:5 CEV

Every morning is a chance at a new day.

MARJORIE HINCKLEY

DaySpring

WHAT A GIFT YOU ARE TO THIS DAY, THIS WEEK, THIS LIFE, THIS WORLD. THANKING GOD FOR YOU!

Let's celebrate and be glad today.

PSALM 118:24 CEV

Gratitude therefore takes nothing for granted, is never unresponsive, is constantly awakening to new wonder and to praise of the goodness of God.

THOMAS MERTON

DaySpring

I prayed that you would intensely feel His love and grasp the *reality of His grace* today—so much so that your heart is filled with awe and thanks.

TEACH US TO REALIZE THE BREVITY OF LIFE, SO THAT WE MAY GROW IN WISDOM.

PSALM 90:12 NLT

The earth under your feet, the rain over your face upturned, the stars spinning all around you in the brazen glory: this is for you, you, you. These are for you . . . so count the ways He loves, a thousand, more, never stop.

ANN VOSKAMP

DaySpring

THANKING GOD TODAY FOR HOW **HE HAS SHOWN UP** AND SHONE OUT IN YOUR LIFE.

This is how God showed His love to us: He sent His one and only Son into the world so that we could have life through Him.

I JOHN 4:9 NCV

This is one of those days when we can look back, taste, see, and know that God is good and love is winning.

SARAH MUELLER

DaySpring

I thanked God today for holding your hand and staying *by your side today* and for the years to come.

NO DOUBT ABOUT IT!

GOD IS GOOD.

PSALM 73:1 THE MESSAGE

Be still, and in the quiet moments, listen to the voice of your heavenly Father. His words can renew your spirit. No one knows you and your needs like He does.

JANET L. SMITH

DaySpring

OH, HOW GOD LOVES YOU.

OH, HOW HE CARES.

I'M PRAYING THAT YOU WOULD FEEL YOUR PLACE IN HIS HEART DEEPLY TODAY.

How I praise the Lord.

PHILIPPIANS 4:10 NLT

When you walk . . . God will steady you.
When you run . . . He will sustain you.
And when you fly . . . yes, when you fly—
He will take you places you never dreamed.

LINN CARLSON

DaySpring

Asking God to show you His fatherly love today, in all the ways *you need it most.*

BUT THOSE WHO TRUST IN THE LORD WILL FIND NEW STRENGTH. THEY WILL SOAR HIGH ON WINGS LIKE EAGLES. THEY WILL RUN AND NOT GROW WEARY. THEY WILL WALK AND NOT FAINT.

ISAIAH 40:31 NLT

For God is, indeed, a wonderful Father who longs to pour out His mercy upon us, and whose majesty is so great that He can transform us from deep within.

MOTHER TERESA

DaySpring

YOU'VE BEEN **FAITHFUL AND TRUE, STRONG AND COURAGEOUS.** I'M THANKING GOD FOR LEADING YOU THROUGH AND ASKING HIM TO BLESS YOU DEEPLY.

Create in me a clean heart, O God; and renew a steadfast spirit within me.

PSALM 51:10 NKJV

You who have received so much love, share it with others. Love others the way that God has loved you, with tenderness.

MOTHER TERESA

DaySpring

Praying that God's unfailing love would fill your heart with deep and lasting *gratitude.*

DEAR FRIENDS, SINCE GOD LOVED US THAT MUCH, WE SURELY OUGHT TO LOVE EACH OTHER. NO ONE HAS EVER SEEN GOD. BUT IF WE LOVE EACH OTHER, GOD LIVES IN US, AND HIS LOVE IS BROUGHT TO FULL EXPRESSION IN US.

I JOHN 4:11–12 NLT

God is not only the answer to a thousand needs, He is also the answer to a thousand wants. He is the fulfillment of our chief desire in all of life. For whether or not we've ever recognized it, what we desire is unfailing love.

BETH MOORE

DaySpring

GOD'S LOVE FOR YOU IS REAL AND HIS HOPES FOR YOU ARE HIGH. I'M PRAYING YOU RECOGNIZE **HOW AMAZING YOUR UNIQUENESS AND BEAUTY ARE TO THE WORLD!**

GOD promises to love me all day, sing songs all through the night! My life is God's prayer.

PSALM 42:8 THE MESSAGE

You are God's created beauty and the focus of His affection and delight.

JANET WEAVER SMITH

DaySpring

Thanking God for your beautiful heart *and generous spirit.* You truly are a gift!

YOU SHOULD CLOTHE YOURSELVES
INSTEAD WITH THE BEAUTY
THAT COMES FROM WITHIN,
THE UNFADING BEAUTY OF
A GENTLE AND QUIET SPIRIT,
WHICH IS SO PRECIOUS TO GOD.

I PETER 3:4 NLT

We are dreamed up in God's heart, formed by His hands, and placed in this world for a purpose.

HOLLEY GERTH

DaySpring

AS I PRAY FOR YOU TODAY,
I'M THANKING GOD
FOR THE PURPOSE
HE'S GIVEN YOU
AND THE POTENTIAL
THAT SPARKS OUT OF YOU
EVERY TIME YOU
OPERATE IN YOUR GIFTS
AND PASSIONS.

We know that in all things God works for the good of those who love Him, who have been called according to His purpose.

ROMANS 8:28 NIV

You were made ON purpose, FOR a purpose.

TONY EVANS

DaySpring

Praying that today you are able to rest in the knowledge that God has it *all figured out.*

TAKE DELIGHT IN THE LORD AND
HE WILL GIVE YOU THE DESIRES OF YOUR HEART.
COMMIT YOUR WAY TO THE LORD;
TRUST IN HIM AND HE WILL DO THIS:
HE WILL MAKE YOUR RIGHTEOUS REWARD SHINE
LIKE THE DAWN, YOUR VINDICATION
LIKE THE NOONDAY SUN.

PSALM 37:4–6 NIV

I may have a "To Do" list for today,
but my "To Be" list comes first.
Be still. Be grateful. Be content. Be loved.

MATT ANDERSON

DaySpring

LIFE IS NOT ALWAYS EASY,
BUT REMEMBER THIS:
**GOD KNOWS, HE SEES,
HE UNDERSTANDS,
AND HE LOVES.**
PRAYING YOU FEEL
HIS DEEP LOVE TODAY.

**Pray without ceasing;
in everything give thanks;
for this is God's will for you
in Christ Jesus.**

I THESSALONIANS 5:17–18 NASB

The place where we find contentment has no earthly address. It's that supernatural spot where we realize the infinite treasures of heaven are already ours.

ANONYMOUS

DaySpring

As I pray for you today, I'm asking God to give you the time, room, and space to *rest in His grace.*

HE SAYS, "BE STILL, AND KNOW THAT I AM GOD; I WILL BE EXALTED AMONG THE NATIONS, I WILL BE EXALTED IN THE EARTH." THE LORD ALMIGHTY IS WITH US; THE GOD OF JACOB IS OUR FORTRESS.

PSALM 46:10–11 NIV

The inwards fortitude needed to face life's difficulties comes only as we open our hearts to Christ in the quiet moment, ceasing from activity and letting Him supply guidance, confidence, and direction as we reflect on His Word.

DR. DAVID JEREMIAH

DaySpring

WITH GOD, ALL THINGS **ARE POSSIBLE!** NOTHING IS TOO HARD FOR HIM. I ASKED GOD TO GUIDE YOU AS YOU TAKE THESE EXCITING, NEW STEPS IN YOUR LIFE.

Then the word of the LORD came to Jeremiah, saying, "Behold, I am the LORD, the God of all flesh. Is there anything too hard for Me?"

JEREMIAH 32:26–27 NKJV

For little things . . . for big things . . . for all things . . . there is room in the heart to be thankful.

BONNIE JENSEN

DaySpring

Praying for you today! God's plans for you *are perfect,* and His dreams for you are amazing!

TRUST IN THE LORD WITH ALL YOUR HEART AND LEAN NOT ON YOUR OWN UNDERSTANDING; IN ALL YOUR WAYS SUBMIT TO HIM, AND HE WILL MAKE YOUR PATHS STRAIGHT.

PROVERBS 3:5–6 NIV

God wants us to move through this day with a quiet heart, an inward assurance that He is in control, a peaceful certainty that your life is in His hands.

ROY LESSIN

DaySpring